I0439909

Absolute Crime Presents:

Delivery of Death

The Shocking Story of the Ranong

Human-Trafficking Incident

ABSO UTE
CR ME

By Reagan Martin

Absolute Crime Books

www.absolutecrime.com

© 2013. All Rights Reserved.

Cover Image © andreykr - Fotolia.com

Table of Contents

About Us

Absolute Crime publishes only the best true crime literature. Our focus is on the crimes that you've probably never heard of, but you are fascinated to read more about. With each engaging and gripping story, we try to let readers relive moments in history that some people have tried to forget.

Remember, our books are not meant for the faint at heart. We don't hold back—if a crime is bloody, we let the words splatter across the page so you can experience the crime in the most horrifying way!

If you enjoy this book, please visit our homepage to see other books we offer; if you have any feedback, we'd love to hear from you!

Prologue

Thiry-two year old Ko Hla pulled his nineteen year old girlfriend closer, and managed a brave smile as they surveyed the small compartment of the refrigerated truck. He could feel the girl trembling at his side, her teeth chattering softly as if she had caught a chill, and he instinctively squeezed her tighter. He knew that she was not cold, only apprehensive, as she had been ever since leaving their native Burma to begin this long journey. Now, seeing the actual container of the truck, Ko was feeling anxious himself, although he was careful not to let his girlfriend know.

The truck compartment was tiny; much tinier than he had ever imagined it would be. Ko estimated that it couldn't measure more than 20 feet in length, and maybe 6 feet in width. Glancing around at the group of people who stood with him, he wondered how they would ever fit. The truck looked like it would have trouble carrying fifty people comfortably, let alone this crowd. Although Ko didn't know how many people were milling about with him, it certainly appeared to be a lot more than that, maybe even as many as 85 to 100.

The exact number of those about to embark on this passage with Ko Hla was 120, to be precise, and the young man was correct in his thinking. There was absolutely no way they would ever fit comfortably inside this small container.

Ko had not seen the driver of the truck, who would be responsible for transporting them to what they hoped would be good jobs and a better life, but a man and woman who had met them on the pier were there, walking amongst the waiting crowd, hastening them on.

'Hurry, hurry', they urged, 'climb up, get in. **Hurry**.'

The throng began to move towards the container, and Ko and his girlfriend were pushed along, inching closer and closer to the vehicle, which sat with its engine running. They pulled themselves up into the compartment, and as the rest of the waiting people struggled to climb aboard the two were forced to move further towards the front.

It was pitch black inside the truck box, and as Ko and his girl sat down, people kept coming, squeezing the couple closer and closer together until they were packed like sardines inside the stifling hot compartment.

Soon space in the tiny trailer ran out, and people were forced to sit on top of each other. Ko noticed a woman and child sitting near him, the woman holding the little girl on her lap, trying to soothe her. But no matter how much she cooed to the girl and whispered to her, Ko could see that it wasn't helping. The child appeared to be absolutely terrified.

After what seemed like an eternity the truck doors finally swung closed, and Ko could feel the vehicle begin to move. It shifted gears and slowly accelerated, rumbling along the invisible street outside.

The inside of the container was cloistered, terrifying in the inky black darkness, and sweltering hot. The sweat began to bead on Ko's forehead, and then seep out along the flesh of his arms. Soon it was running down his body in rivulets, soaking through his clothing and saturating his hair. It beaded up on the ends of each strand, dripping down into his eyes and creating a burning sensation that he was unable to relieve. The back of the truck was so tightly jammed with people it was nearly impossible for him to raise his hand just to wipe his eyes.

The others crammed into that tiny space were feeling the same way as Ko. Many of them desperately tried to shift position, an endeavor that was not only futile, but one which angered those sitting nearby. Several were beginning to cry, as their inability to do anything about their miserable situation increased their frustration. But it was what Ko heard next that really frightened him.

People were beginning to moan and wheeze, apparently gasping for air and unable to catch their breath. Several were muttering that they couldn't breathe. The little girl sitting on her mother's lap was crying and begging for help.

A dim glow began to penetrate the darkness as people lit lighters in a vain attempt to see. In the shadowy light, Ko could barely discern the appalling conditions, and the other anxious faces peering around. But it obvious that they were all in serious trouble, and he wondered how long would it be before panic set in.

In a desperate effort to get help, the people began to bang on the walls of the container, screaming for the truck driver to stop. They yelled and they pounded, using energy they couldn't afford to spare, but their calls went unheeded.

Although those inside the truck weren't aware of it, one man in their group had been provided with a cell phone and the number of the driver earlier in the evening. He quickly attempted to call the man, but he was panicked himself, and in the dark he fumbled with the phone, nearly dropping it. Willing himself to calm down, the man finally completed his call and was relieved when the driver answered. Nearly shouting, he begged him to stop the truck, telling him that there was no air inside and they were unable to breathe.

But the vehicle did not stop. It continued on its way, much to the dismay of those inside, and the moaning and gasping continued. And then, suddenly, there was a loud hissing noise, and cool, frosty air began to flow into the trailer. The driver hadn't stopped, but he had turned on the refrigeration unit, bringing immediate relief and joy to those trapped inside.

Ko said a mental prayer of thanks as he smiled down at his girlfriend. Then, unable to resist, he kissed the top of her head and nuzzled her sopping wet hair. The others inside began to laugh and to shout, delighted, happy, and blissfully unaware that the relief would be only temporary.

Chapter One

Ko Hla and his girlfriend, as well as the others riding in the back of the truck, were from the country of Burma, or Myanmar, a sovereign state in Southeast Asia. Their country had been under military control since 1962, and conditions there were harsh, as well as brutal. Well known for its inhumane treatment against its own people, the government of Burma subjected its citizens not only to horrendous living conditions, but also to genocide, child labor, slavery, repeated rapes of their women, and unbelievable poverty.

As a result of these gross human rights violations, and in an effort to escape them, thousands of Burmese people began to look elsewhere, hoping to find some place that would provide a better future for them. Between 1962, and 1988 a slow trickle of Burmese citizens migrated to other countries to start a new life.

But in 1988, when the Burmese Socialist Regime collapsed, it left its people out of work, destitute, and with no way to feed their families. In an effort to survive, millions more from the country of Myanmar were forced to flee, leaving all their worldly possessions to seek work elsewhere.

Although Burma is bordered by five different countries, Thailand, China, Laos, India, and Bangladesh, it was to Thailand that the majority of the Burmese people fled. The country was close by and reminiscent of home, and the border between Burma and Thailand was the Kra Buri River, making passage between the two countries easy. But more importantly, Thailand offered greater opportunities than Burma's others neighbors.

Many of these Burmese migrants entered Thailand in the city of Ranong, a small fishing port that bordered the Kra Buri River. Ranong was a center for the fishing and seafood industries, and in the year 2008, it had a population of 300,000. Nearly half of the city's residents were made up of Burmese migrants.

These migrants had come to Thailand hoping to find work and make a better life for themselves, and fortunately, for some, they would realize that dream. But for many others, the dream would quickly turn into a nightmare.

****

The government of Thailand, like most countries, was not receptive to welcoming millions of illegal immigrants crossing their borders. But unlike many other countries, Thailand had a great need for these alien bodies, and they knew it. The southern part of the country, with its beautiful beaches and balmy climate, was quickly becoming a major tourist destination, and growth in the area was rapid. And, as with any advancement, help was desperately needed.

There were jobs open for everyone; construction workers to build high rise hotels, and maids to clean them. People to work in the fish industry and on agricultural farms, ensuring there was enough food available to feed those who came to vacation. And of course women, young, sultry and sexy females, to pleasure those lonely souls who traveled there.

There was so much work in fact that the country couldn't provide enough manpower to fill the need. More and more often, the Thais would turn to migrants, both legal and illegal, to satisfy the demand. The migrants were hard working, discreet, and extremely cheap labor.

In December of 2004, when Thailand was hit by the great tsunami that resulted from the Indian Ocean earthquake, the southern part of the country was left in ruins. In the small resort areas around Ranong and Phuket, nearly 2600 people were killed, and the devastation was vast. Thailand desperately needed workers to re-build, and the Burmese migrants were eager to fill this need.

But without the Thai Government allowing them to legally enter the country, the people of Myanmar had no way to get in. Desperate to work and have money to feed their families, the majority of them were forced to turn to migrant brokers; men and women who offered to smuggle them into the country for a fee. To many of these desperate Burmese souls, finding a job broker seemed like a godsend. But in reality, it was not.

****

Whenever desperate circumstances arise, evil and greedy people are right there to seize the opportunity. They make their living preying on the vulnerabilities and desperate hopes of troubled and worried individuals, and the job brokers that many Burmese people turned to were no exception.

Migrant brokering is organized crime at its worst. A huge business, it generates millions of dollars in profit each year, and destroys just as many lives. It begins with the broker collecting a hefty fee, anywhere from 6,000 to 12,000 baht, (the equivalent of $180 to $360 U.S. dollars), to smuggle the illegal immigrant out of the country and secure him a job.

Since it was obvious that the typical migrant could never come up with that kind of money before he left the country, it was common for an arrangement to be agreed upon whereby the migrant would pay off his debt to the broker in installments. It seemed like the perfect arrangement, except that once the migrants were inside Thailand and working, they were quick to discover that they had blindly dug themselves into a hole they could never get out of.

Like others who desperately want something, and will agree to just about anything to get it, the migrants too rarely thought about the consequences of what they were agreeing to. They didn't consider the fact that they would be paid far less than the Thai natives, nor did they ever contemplate the price they were paying for their freedom. A broker's fee could be as high as 12,000 baht per person. For a lone migrant, this could take years to pay off, but for a family, with two or four children, the debt could last a lifetime.

But it was not only the broker that the migrant owed fees to, the police and military demanded a share of his wages as well. If the migrant didn't want to face criminal charges as an illegal alien, spend time in prison, be ordered to pay a fine, and then be deported back to his native country, he would have to pay.

Too late, many of those who came into the country illegally quickly realized that often their living conditions here were worse than they had been at home. After all the payouts, there was no money left to buy decent food, clothing or medical care.

The Burmese migrants also found that working conditions could be extremely harsh. For example, those who took jobs on a fishing vessel found that they were out to sea for thirty to forty days at a stretch, with only a three to five day respite in port. For this work, the migrant would be paid 3,000 to 6,000 baht per month, ($90 to $180 US dollars), while the Thai doing the same job on the same boat was paid double that. When he finally did get a few days off at home, he was too tired to spend it with his family, finding that he slept most of the time before returning to the ship.

Those migrants who went to work on farms found their working conditions pretty much the same as those on the fishing vessels. They worked long days, in sweltering heat, for very little money. The only exception was that they were allowed to be home each night.

Even worse than the fishing and farming industries were those who took jobs in factories. These migrants found themselves working in sweatshops, toiling from 12 to 14 hours each day for little more than $50 to $75 dollars a month.

There was another routine in their new country that greatly upset the immigrants; the practice of their new employers to confiscate their passports. Ordered to release them upon being hired, this action made it impossible for the migrants to quit their jobs, or leave the country, even if they wanted to.

After only a few weeks in their new home, many of those who had come seeking a brighter future found themselves saddled with debt, living in a foreign country, and missing the one thing that could get them home; their passports.

For Ko Hla and all the others riding in the small container of that miserable seafood truck, the chance that they were heading into this very same situation, although not thought about by them, was a distinct possibility.

Chapter Two

For all the ways that life in a new country had not lived up to the migrant's expectations, they found that they had a far bigger problem that overshadowed everything else. They were extremely vulnerable to human trafficking.

The distinction between migrant smuggling and human trafficking can often be difficult to determine. Very similar in nature, the only real difference between the two are consent, exploitation, and profit.

Those who hire a job broker and request to be smuggled out of a country are giving their consent. Their entire ordeal is supposed to end once their destination is reached. The profit made from this act comes from the transportation fee paid by the migrant, or by the money he pays to ensure his stay in the country.

On the other hand, a person who finds himself a victim of human trafficking is typically put into this position by means of force, threat, deception, coercion, or abuse of power. Upon reaching their destination, their ordeal doesn't end, but in fact is just beginning. They are no longer allowed any choices, are not free to leave, and are exploited by others in order for them to make a profit. These migrants might be forced to work as prostitutes, sold into slavery or forced labor, and even, at times, murdered to remove and sell their internal organs.

Although the two seem like different and distinct environments, migrant smuggling can quickly turn into human trafficking without the victim even knowing it. For instance, the migrant who paid the broker to smuggle him out of Burma and then took a job on the fishing boat is technically a smuggled immigrant. However, his being forced to work for abysmally low wages in order to pay off his broker's transportation fee is a form or coercion. Thus, without even being aware of it, this same man has moved from the category of smuggled migrant to human trafficking victim.

At other times trafficking is the intent all along, but the broker might approach the migrant and request a fee to gain his consent and trust. Because the immigrant initially agrees, it might look like a case of smuggling when all along the person was actually a victim of human trafficking.

On other occasions, the intent truly is only to smuggle, but if the broker finds himself faced with a lucrative opportunity to traffic the people instead, he will usually accept it. Human trafficking generates tens of billions of dollars in profits each year, and those involved in it are paid very well.

****

Victims of human trafficking include people of all ages and genders, but the vast majority of them are women. Seventy-nine percent of the estimated 2.5 million victims of human trafficking are being used for sexual exploitation. Many young girls are simply kidnapped off the streets and forced to work as prostitutes. But for others, their initiation into the world of the sex trade business came from people they knew and trusted.

One young Myanmar girl tells the story of being approached by a Burmese woman, who offered her a job as a maid in one of the fine hotels in the vacation town of Phuket. The woman assured her that the working conditions were exceptional, and she could expect to make a salary of about $950 a month, which included the tips she would receive from the rich people who stayed there. This was an astronomical amount of money for a poor Myanmar family, and the girl, only fifteen years old, readily accepted. She knew she could live on less than $200 a month, and would then be able to send the remaining money back to her struggling parents.

The fact that the job offer came from a female, and a fellow Myanmar, put the young girl at ease. She was not aware that most human traffickers prey on their own nationality, nor did she know that a large number of these predators are women who were once trafficked themselves. In an effort to escape their own plight, many females turn to the same crime that had victimized them in the first place.

When the young girl arrived in Thailand expecting to go to work in a hotel in Phuket she was instead kept in the city of Ranong and immediately locked away in small room for days on end. She saw no one, spoke to no one, and even her food, little more than a bowl of rice each day, was carefully placed on the floor just inside her door.

After about a week, the door to her prison opened and two men stood outside staring at her. One was young, while the other was a much older gentleman, probably somewhere in his mid to late sixties. The young man gestured at the girl, and then told the older man that the cost for 'opening a Burmese package' would be 13,000 baht. The old man nodded, handed the younger man a wad of bills, and then entered the room. The young man departed, pulled the door shut, and locked it from the outside.

Terrified, the young girl lay motionless as the older man ravished and raped her, panting and sweating as he nearly crushed her beneath him. When he was finally finished, the old man had laughed and then told her that 'opening a Burmese package' was a euphemism for having sex with a virgin Myanmar girl.

The ritual remained the same for the young girl month after month. She stayed locked away in the little room and was forced to have sex with dozens of strange men. Eventually her captors brought her out of her prison and put her to work in a Ranong brothel.

One day, seeing a rare opportunity, she fled from the house and flagged down a passing policeman. Begging him to help her, the officer instead returned her to the brothel, where she was stripped naked, repeatedly raped, and then viciously beaten.

This was not an unusual occurrence. Many of those in authority were blatantly corrupt and involved in the human trafficking trade for profit. Undoubtedly, the police officer who returned the girl to the brothel was paid handsomely by the owners to do so.

Had this policeman not been corrupt, the young girl's fate would not have been all that much better. She would certainly not have been viewed as a victim, but instead as criminal, guilty of illegal entry into the country, and most likely thrown in jail.

Before human trafficking became a well-known word, officials had little understanding of the difference between smuggling, trafficking, and migration. They viewed anyone in the country illegally, no matter how they came to be there, as criminals. Hauled into jail and placed in cells, they would be tried, sentenced to prison, given a stiff fine, and then deported back to their native countries. But most of the time their own country didn't want them back, and they were left with no money and no place to go. To many, their situation was hopeless.

But for the young prostitute who had tried to escape and failed, the isolation, humiliation, and terror eventually did its job. Just as her kidnappers knew she would, the girl yielding to her plight, and did what she was told. She never complained, cried, or tried to fight. And she never again attempted to escape.

But despite the fact that she was a model slave, turning tricks for her captors for nearly twelve hours a day, she received no money, and was never able to send her parents a dime. The other girls working with her explained that she would not make any money until she paid back what the brothel owners had spent to purchase her.

The young girl never saw the Burmese woman who had brought her to Thailand again, and her story, or ones exactly like it, are a dime a dozen. Some victims of human trafficking are never released from their bondage, often because death takes them first. Others, mainly the old or the injured, those who are of little value anymore, will sometimes be allowed to 'buy' their freedom. But the price is steep, and for thousands, nearly impossible to attain.

And for almost all of them, there is little hope of rescue. If this young girls parents ever managed to look for her, they would do so in Phuket, never knowing that they were looking in the wrong place. It was a standard ruse that the traffickers came to know worked very well.

****

For many of these slaves, their journey began the same way Ko Hla's had; in the small, cramped compartments of delivery trucks hired to carry them, and their hopes for a better future to destinations unknown.

Many had agreed to pay a price to leave their country, just like those now barreling down the highway trapped within the confines of the seafood trailer had. So, were Ko Hla and his group truly smuggled migrants, or were they too victims of human trafficking? The answer to that question remained to be seen.

Chapter Three

As the seafood truck continued to travel through the streets of Ranong, those locked inside did their best to ignore their uncomfortable surroundings. At least they could breathe a little easier now that there was finally some cool air flowing in from the refrigeration unit.

Other than some rustling and a few dry coughs, the container was mainly quiet, most of the migrants lost in thoughts of the life they were leaving behind and the new one they hoped to begin. Ko Hla sat with his eyes closed, concentrating on the events that had led him to this moment in time.

He had paid a migrant broker 12,000 baht to secure not only his entry into Thailand, but also a job in the resort city of Phuket, where major construction was underway. Phuket had been hard hit by the tsunami five years earlier, but it was a popular destination for tourists so re-building had been quick to begin. The new construction, however, was to be state of the art, not only beautiful, but also able to withstand the power of another tidal wave.

Hla, his girlfriend, and several others in the truck had made their way to Victoria Point, a Burmese town across the river from Ranong, where they were joined by more Myanmar citizens from other villages. All had paid a job broker to organize this trip for them.

Each was then hidden in the hold of a large cargo ship, another miserable and suffocating compartment, until sometime during the evening of April 8, 2008, when they sailed over to Thailand. The crossing had been uneventful, but upon docking, they were told they must remain in the cargo hold for another 24 hours. This announcement was greeted by sighs, moans, and outright curses.

Finally, around 7:00 pm, on April 9, 2008, they were allowed to leave the hold and come up on deck where they were immediately ushered onto the Choke Charoen fishing pier. A 10-wheeled truck, carrying a white, twenty foot long, unventilated seafood container was backed up to the pier, the doors of the trailer hanging open. Soon, a man and woman were urging them to get into the container, and to hurry.

Now, Ko Hla had been riding in that same container for the past hour. He knew the trip to Phuket would take about four hours total, and he hoped he could hang on that long. Already his legs were cramping, tingling, giving the annoying sensation that they had fallen asleep. He could hardly move an inch, his head throbbed and his back ached.

Someone nearby lit their lighter, casting an eerie glow in his immediate vicinity, and Ko noticed the woman with the child still on her lap. The little girl appeared to have fallen asleep, and Hla envied her. He wished he could fall asleep and escape this ride from hell.

The truck continued to rumble along, and those inside, although barely aware of the hiss of the compressor that released the cool, breathable air, knew immediately when it stopped working. There was no noise to indicate it, no bang or clank, but the hissing sound ceased abruptly, and there was no one who failed to notice it.

There were moans, and groans, and curses from the migrants, one lady muttering 'Oh, no," while another added sarcastically 'Well that's just great!'

The entire compartment seemed to rock and shimmy, as everyone came alert, moving and shifting, trying to figure out what had happened.

'Call the driver,' someone shouted.

But others in the truck were quick to veto the suggestion, telling the man with the phone, 'no, not yet'. They didn't want to make the driver angry, or seem like complainers. They thought it possible that he couldn't run the compressor the whole time, and if they just waited patiently, he'd turn it back on in a few minutes.

The others in the container didn't argue, and things quieted down for the moment. The man with the phone, who had taken it out and was ready to dial, took it as a silent agreement to wait.

****

Up front, sitting behind the wheel in the cab of the truck, thirty-eight year old Suchon Bunplong, like the migrants he was hauling, was also lost in thought. He was thinking about the events that led him to be driving a truck loaded with 120 illegal immigrants, and wishing that this trip were already over.

According to what he would later tell authorities, Suchon had been hired to do the job by a man named Damrong Phussadee, the owner of the seafood truck, and was paid 80,000 baht, ($2400 U.S. dollars) for the job. He had already received half of the payment up front, and was expected to receive the balance once he delivered his cargo in Phuket.

Suchon had been instructed to meet with a man and woman at the Choke Charoen fishing pier and pick up the truck there. The owner of the pier, Jirawat Sophapanworagul, was married to a woman who had been arrested in 1996 on a charge of human trafficking, although it is unclear whether Suchon knew about this. Also unclear was whether the man and woman he met on the pier were the Sophoapanworagul's.

Regardless, after leaving the pier with his human cargo, the woman had phoned him numerous times asking if everything was okay, and if he was sure the people had enough air in the back of the truck.

Suchon, although assuring her that all was well each time she called, was never the less annoyed to find that she continued to phone anyway. He didn't bother to tell her about the unexpected phone call he received, from one of the migrants in the back of the truck, telling him they couldn't breathe. Instead, he immediately turned on the trucks refrigeration system and all had quieted down.

But his thoughts were no longer on the woman and her phone calls, or the events that had led him to this moment in time. Instead, for the past twenty minutes, it had taken all of Bunplong's concentration just to negotiate the winding and twisting road in front of him. He had been driving for about an hour now, and the street was dark and narrow. Blind curves and numerous bends kept his eyes peeled open and his hands clenching the wheel. The man was nervous, on edge, and the fact that his cell phone just kept ringing didn't make matters any easier.

Whether Bunplong realized that the cooling system in the back of the truck had failed is not known. But what is known is that as the drive became more treacherous, and the phone continued to ring, he simply stopped answering it.

****

Within twenty minutes of the compressor shutting down, those trapped in the seafood container were sweating profusely, and beginning to have trouble catching their breath. The stench in the cramped compartment was enough to turn even the most hardened stomachs. It was the sickening sweet odor of human sweat, despair, and fear.

The little girl who lay in her mother's lap was no longer sleeping, and Ko Hla could hear her gasping for air. She kept pleading with her mother to help, telling her that she couldn't breathe. The mother was doing what she could, but she was crying and gasping for air herself.

Others in the truck were moaning and thrashing, crying out that they were burning up and unable to breath. Some began to shout, screaming at the man with the phone to call the driver. The man did so, repeatedly, but he never received an answer.

****

As Suchon maneuvered the truck through the inky black night, his cell phone continued to ring, shrilling out its tone every few minutes. Within a short amount of time, the ring tone remained constant, with barely a one second pause between each call. Frustrated, and with his nerves at their end, Suchon Bunplong reached over and turned the phone off.

****

Conditions in the cargo container of the truck were deteriorating rapidly. People appeared to be delirious now, calling out long phrases that made absolutely no sense. One man began struggling to get up, hitting and clawing at those jammed in next to him, shouting that he had vegetables in the garden that needed attending.

The heat in the container was brutal, blistering, and suffocating. People began peeling off their clothes, throwing them around, causing others to begin screaming at them in anger.

Soon, people were vomiting and choking, creating more vile odors to go along with the stench that was nearly unbearable. Within minutes the acrid smell of urine was added to the fray, permeating the air and making it difficult to even attempt a breath.

The little girl was no longer pleading for help, but her mother was moaning, and then wailing, squeezing the child tightly in her arms. Ko Hla was finding it hard to think straight or catch his breath. His temples pounded, and there were sounds and words and screams all jumbled in his head. He felt dizzy, disoriented and out of touch.

But suddenly, in the midst of all this chaos, Ko Hla heard the little girl's mother distinctly; and what he heard her saying chilled him to the bone.

"She's dead." The mother moaned, "My little girl is dead."

These words brought several in the truck to immediate attention. Now, more alert than they had been, they could hear others screaming and wailing about death and dying. The man with the cell phone was sobbing, telling the others that his calls were going directly to voice mail, an indication that the driver's phone had been shut off.

Ko Hla knew that they had to get out of this truck or they were all doomed. He began to bang against the side of the container, screaming for the driver to stop. Others joined in, pounding, banging, screaming at the top of their lungs, until the little white container was practically jostling from side to side.

****

Suchon Bunplong was startled to feel the truck container literally sway behind him, and then hear the screaming and banging emanating from it. He knew there was a problem back there, but he didn't know how serious it was. He was reluctant to stop for fear that it would arouse suspicion from passing motorists.

He continued to drive on, hoping that the migrants would settle down, but the ruckus from the container just continued to get louder and louder. Only a few miles up ahead there was a military checkpoint and Bunplong worried about approaching it. Typically, officials there needed only to see a 500 baht banknote and they would allow you to pass. But Suchon was certain that this time, the uproar in the container would not be ignored.

Reluctantly, he finally pulled his vehicle to the side of the road and got out. Moving to the back of the container, he unlocked the two doors and pulled them open. The migrants were packed so tightly inside that several of them tumbled out onto the pavement once the doors swung open.

Immediately, before Suchon could even look inside, more and more people were jumping from the container, gasping for air and falling to the ground. Finally, when it seemed all were out, Suchon peered into the compartment. What he saw made the blood in his veins run cold. He stared for a moment, horrified yet transfixed, and shivering despite the heat of the evening. And then he took off, abandoning the truck and its cargo, and fleeing the scene as fast he could.

Chapter Four

Around 10:30 pm, on the evening of April 9, 2008, the police of Ranong began receiving phone calls about a 10-wheeled white seafood truck abandoned on the side of the road in Village 3.

Responding to the scene, authorities were shocked by what they found. There were people milling all around the back of the truck, and several lying on the ground. Some looked to be unconscious, while others appeared delirious, crying and moaning, and sometimes even fighting while people tried to attend to them. Everyone seemed to be hysterical, and as the police approached, many rushed at them, all attempting to speak at the same time. While some officers tried to calm the frantic crowd, others climbed aboard the seafood container.

The first thing that hit them was the pungent odor coming from inside. It assaulted their senses, a foul, bitter combination of urine, body fluids, vomit, and dead fish. Shining their flashlights around, they were greeted by a grisly sight that stopped them in their tracks.

Clothing littered the floor and draped the bodies that were strewn all over the truck bed. They were sprawled in a jumble, contorted and twisted, some on top of each other, others remaining in the same seated position they had traveled in. One witness would later say that upon seeing the sight, he was immediately reminded of the aerial photos he had seen of the Jonestown Massacre in Guyana, the colored clothing scattered about and bodies piled on top of one another.

Stepping farther inside, the officers called to those lying motionless on the floor, nudging some with their feet, and bending to inspect others. There was no response from any of them, and it soon became apparent that those left inside were all dead.

There was a doctor on the scene, and the ambulances were called. Police watched as they rushed ten of those lying on the ground to area hospitals. Originally, when the news of the tragedy was made public, police would claim that 121 people had been in the truck. Days later, however, they would amend this count when they learned that one of those taken to the hospital was actually a Thai citizen who had fainted at the gruesome sight.

Incredibly, after the ambulances had left, police placed the other fifty-seven survivors under arrest and hauled them off to jail. Each was charged with illegally entering the country, and housed in prison cells overnight.

Inside the truck container authorities found fifty-four dead bodies; seventeen men, thirty-six women, and the eight year old little girl who had begged her mom for help.

****

After peering into the cargo bed of his truck and seeing the death and destruction that lay inside, Suchon Bunplong had panicked. With his heart pounding and his head spinning he immediately fled the scene, running as fast as his legs could carry him.

Eventually, he found a set of low-lying bushes and crawled under them, where he curled himself into a ball and hid. He was in a state of disbelief, shocked, panicked, and shivering with fear. By dawn he had calmed down enough to know that he couldn't hide forever. Emerging from the bushes, he walked to the nearest highway and began hitchhiking, quickly catching a ride to the Kapoe District.

Once there, he boarded a bus to Chumphon, getting off in the Lang Suan District. Later that evening he travelled to Nakhon Si Thammarat and then Bangkok, where he rented a motel room and watched the drama he was responsible for unfold on TV. He could hardly believe what he was hearing, and found it hard to look when they showed photos of the scene. Guilt ridden and deeply shamed, he wondered what to do.

****

Not surprisingly, when news broke of the suffocation deaths of fifty-four people being smuggled in the back of a sealed container, it produced a media storm throughout Thailand and the world. The story would go on to become the single most important event responsible for bringing the crime of human trafficking to the knowledge of the general public. It would also propel the country of Thailand into the spotlight, and create an international furor over the country's treatment of illegal immigrants.

Thai officials tried to do damage control by claiming that the country's problem with illegal aliens was one that the government was working on daily. In fact, they stressed, the Thai Prime Minister had recently suggested creating an Island Detention Center in the Adaman Sea to provide shelter for the illegals, and serve as a deterrent to others wanting to enter. As long as migrants avoided the legal channels needed to enter the country, they said, tragedies such as this were bound to happen.

****

Meanwhile, police continued their investigation into the entire event. The seafood truck had Ranong license plates, and was registered to Rungruengsup Limited Partnership. It was owned by a man named Damrong Phussadee, but as of now authorities had not located him, nor did they know the name of the driver who had also disappeared.

While some of the victims recuperated in the hospital and others languished in a jail cell, the dead were transported to a charity foundation where it was expected they would be buried in a pauper's grave.

To a country whose people are mostly Buddhist, this was devastating news to hear. Burial was the fate of any Buddhist who could not afford cremation at the temple, and it was not viewed as an honorable thing. To those who had survived the tragic event, the announcement felt like adding insult to injury.

****

On April 11, 2008, Damrong Phussadee, the owner of the seafood truck, presented himself to police and agreed to be questioned. He denied any involvement in the smuggling operation, and claimed that he knew nothing about his truck being used for such a criminal affair. Police did not believe him, and placed him under immediate arrest.

On the same day, those men and women who had been taken to jail were due in court. Standing before the bench, looking bedraggled and in a state of shock, the judge decided he needed more time to figure out what he should do with them. Refusing to make a decision on whether they would be tried as illegal immigrants or not, he ordered the group returned to their jail cells.

The next day the Burmese Minister Counselor Myint Soe travelled to Ranong and met with the country's Provincial Governor Kanchanapa Kiman. Kiman first offered Soe and the country of Myanmar her heartfelt condolences for the tragedy, and then quickly assured him that not only would the injured receive free medical care from her country, but she also promised that the truck owner would face 'strong charges' for his role in the crime.

Soe had been ordered by the Burmese government to come to Thailand and investigate the incident, and then report back to them. Soe knew his country was upset by what had happened, but he was also well aware of the Burmese government's reluctance to take back people arrested in Thailand for illegal entry. He was worried about what would happen to the survivors from the seafood truck.

Soe begged Kiman not to press charges against them, but Kiman was not in a position to comment on or give him an answer to his request. Later that day Soe paid a visit to some of the injured still in the hospital and the forty-six others who had been jailed.

That same afternoon, Burmese officials took a Myanmar job broker into custody. The man's name was Kyaw, but whether he was the broker who had arranged this particular trip was not known. Burmese officials declined to elaborate on his arrest.

****

On April 13, 2008, Region 8 Bureau Chief of Police Thani Tawitsri held a press conference that both stunned and angered the country, as well as the entire world.

Claiming that the fifty-four deaths could not be described as human trafficking, he told the news media that his investigation could only make a case against the truck driver, the truck owner, and the sixty-seven survivors of the tragedy.

He went on to say that he would be filing charges against the truck's driver and owner on two separate counts; bringing alien laborers into the Kingdom and giving them assistance and/or shelter, and with negligence causing death. He then added that he intended to charge the survivors with illegal entry into the country.

To say that the announcement caused anger would be an understatement. The news media, as well as the general public, were outraged. Hadn't those fifty-four people gone through enough? Now they were to be tried as common criminals too. People simply couldn't believe it.

On April 14th, in the hopes of doing damage control, the Department of Special Investigation, (DSI), Police Sergeant Suchart Wongananchai, commander of foreign affairs and the international crime office, held his own press conference.

If Thailand refused to enforce the anti-trafficking laws, he said, then the assets of those involved in this case should be confiscated. His investigation had found that these trafficking rings could make 'not less than 100,000 baht' per trip. In his opinion, he continued, when you had this type of 'forced labor smuggling', into a country, and that generated tremendous amounts of money, then it should be viewed as an 'economic crime'. If it were viewed as such, then those involved could, and should, have the freezing of their assets imposed on them.

Suchart had learned that the Burmese victims had paid the job broker anywhere from 8,000 to 12,000 baht each for the job. He also knew that once they were in the country they would be required to pay Thai Government Officials another 10 to 20 baht each, every day, to look the other way.

Suchart emphasized that the survivors should be witnesses in the case, and not 'accused persons', and that the Thailand Government should be responsible for their expenses while they were staying in the country.

Although most people agreed with what Suchart had to say, few of them thought it would actually happen. Needless to say, Thai authorities and Government officials didn't agree with, nor were they happy or impressed by his speech.

****

Meanwhile, Suchon Bunplong, the driver of the truck, was spending his days wandering around in the Sanam Luang district, wracked with guilt. He could not believe that he was responsible for so many people dying, and it haunted him.

Every evening he would return to his hotel room and watch the news coverage of the disaster, becoming more and more depressed and despondent each time he did. But once his mind began to clear and he could think again, little by little his depression was overcome by another emotion; fear.

Bunplong, although not a high-ranking member of any group, was well aware of how far reaching the human trafficking enterprise went. He knew about the billions of dollars that was involved in the trade, and it scared the hell out of him.

What would stop the other members of the ring from killing him to keep him quiet, he wondered? After all, he was the key to the incident, the one who could name names, times, and places. He had the ability to interrupt their entire operation, if not destroy it, within a matter of minutes.

He grappled with the thought of which was worst; becoming a snitch and going to prison, or ending up dead? He knew he would have to make a decision, and he wanted to make it before he was caught. In his search for an answer, he turned to his family. His sister had always helped him in the past; perhaps she could do so again.

Calling her several times, speaking for hours on end, the two siblings finally decided that the best course of action was for Suchon to turn himself in. His sister volunteered to speak to officials and set up the surrender, and Suchon readily agreed.

Chapter Five

The Thai police may have been unable to enforce the anti-trafficking laws in the case of the 120 Burmese migrants, but they certainly knew that human trafficking existed. Not only did it exist, but it was also a major criminal enterprise that was flourishing within their country.

Authorities suspected that the human trafficking ring responsible for bringing the Burmese workers into the country was the Je Ngor gang (Elder Sister Ngor). This was one of five influential groups known to be involved in the human trafficking of Burmese job seekers in the Ranong area. The five groups were a combination of both Thai and Burmese brokers who bribed Thai officials to avoid arrest.

The human trafficking problem in Thailand was more complex than anyone realized at the time. Although all genders were involved, the majority of those being trafficked were young females, brought in for the purpose of working in the sex trade. Some of these girls were forced into prostitution, but for others, those with beautiful faces and lush bodies, the fate was sometimes worse. Many were sold to individual owners, who used them for such things as personal sex slaves, maids, and occasionally punching bags.

But not all of those being trafficked were from other countries, nor were they only female. Many Thai girls, as well as young males from here and abroad, were also forced to work in the sex trade, and compelled to do so by the same means used on others; fear, force, deception, and coercion.

While traffickers could be brutal and heartless, they apparently had no regard for the age of their victims either. Some of those forced to work in the sex trade were as young as six years old. In fact, Thailand's Health System Research Institute reported that even today, 40% of those working as prostitutes in the country of Thailand are children.

One lone female forced into prostitution can provide her trafficker with an income of $250,000 a year. Many will continue to work the girl for years and years, but for others, the sale of the girl outright to another 'pimp' can bring a small fortune in itself. Many 'pimps' (and they are not always men, are more than willing to pay a handsome price for a girl who has already had 'her spirit broken'.

For people forced into a situation, like being ordered to work as a prostitute, the initial reaction for many is defiance. Most, in the beginning, will seize any opportunity to challenge and rebel against their captor. They will fight and defy them at every turn, and desperately try to escape from them. It can take a long time, and a lot of hard work, to transform the woman into a meek and tolerant individual, willing to do just about anything to remain in her captor's good graces.

The methods used to achieve this goal are often ugly and violent, but extremely effective. It requires the systematic brainwashing of an individual, produced by fear, negligence, and savage, brutal beatings. The captor needs the girl to view him as her only means of survival. She must depend on him for all things; the food she eats, the clothes she wears, even the very air she breathes. Traffickers call this 'breaking her spirit', and it is a task that many people find exceptionally distasteful. Thus, potential buyers are willing to pay a tremendous amount of money to have it already done for them.

Like everything else, the sex slave trade in Thailand has ripple down effects. It is a major source of the rampant increase in HIV and AIDS to the country, where an estimated 610,000 people die every year from the deadly disease. And of course, it is also a key contributor to the spread of those less lethal STD's such as gonorrhea and herpes.

From the sex trade to being sold into forced labor, both male and female trafficking victims experience a lot of the same living and working conditions, and they are always held in a financial bondage of indebtedness too.

There were a number of complications that hindered the investigations of human trafficking cases. Prosecuting them was extremely difficult, partly because of the blatant internal corruption of many of those in law enforcement, the government, and the military. A vast number of members from these organizations were not only content to turn their heads and look the other way, but several were also directly involved in the crimes, and took an active role in the incidents.

There was also the fact that most Thai people were not sympathetic to the migrant workers' plight. To the natives, the immigrants were a source of cheap labor who invaded their country and stole work that rightfully belonged to them. Compassion for those held prisoner in a slave trade was not an emotion most Thais were willing to give.

In addition, the lack of understanding as to what human trafficking actually was, and the difficulty in identifying authentic trafficking victims made the crime harder to discern. And the courts of Thailand were well known for their inability to recognize human rights based labor abuse cases.

The main question authorities faced in determining charges against those responsible in the suffocation deaths of the fifty-four Burmese migrant workers was; were they being trafficked at all, or simply smuggled? Where was the evidence of exploitation? Apparently there wasn't any, or at least none that they could prove. Police were quick to point out that each person inside that truck had willingly volunteered to come to Thailand.

****

Even though the police were doing everything in their power to convince the public that this was simply a case of illegal entry that turned tragic, Thailand's Foreign Minister, Noppadon Pattama, urged them to view the incident not only as an illegal immigration crime, but also one of human trafficking. He demanded that those involved be arrested, and that the survivors of the tragedy be treated like victims rather than criminals.

But it did little good. The police eventually announced that it didn't matter what the circumstances might appear to be, there was no way to prove it was a case of human trafficking, and so therefore, it would not be considered as such.

Of course, there was another reason that authorities might have preferred this to be a case of smuggling rather than trafficking. Treating the incident as a smuggling case would speed up the survivor's deportations, and therefore not allow them to stay in Thailand and claim compensation.

****

On April 15, 2008, Suchon Bunplong finally turned himself into the police and confessed his role in the Burmese deaths tragedy. He claimed that it was Damrong Phussadee, the owner of the truck, who had arranged the entire thing and ordered him to pick up the migrants at the Choke Chareon fishing pier.

Bunplong also confessed that he failed to acknowledge his ringing cell phone and the migrants banging on the sides of the truck because he was trying to concentrate on his driving. He then admitted that although he was guilt ridden by what had happened, he had turned himself in mainly out of fear of the other members of his group that he described as a human trafficking ring.

Even with Bunplong's confession in hand, police still insisted they could not bring charges of human trafficking.

Chapter Six

By April 16, 2008, police had three people in custody for the 'death truck incident', as it had come to be called, and had issued warrants for four more. Those already in jail were Suchon Bunplong, the driver, Damrong Phussadee, the truck owner, and Jirawat Sophapanworagul, the owner of the Choke Charoen fishing pier. Police had yet to arrest Weera Dum Yingyaud, Chalhermchai Waritjanpleng, his wife, Panchalee Chusuk, and Supat Phothong. By the very next day, April 17, 2008, authorities had picked up both Waritjanpleng and Yingyaud.

Yingyaud claimed to be Suchon Bunplong's accomplice, and to have ridden with him in the cab of the truck. He told authorities that he had been on several human trafficking runs with Bunplong and was paid 10,000 baht for each one. In addition, he also confessed to being the one who actually opened the truck doors after the migrants had begun screaming and banging on the walls. But he, just like Bunplong, had fled the scene when he realized what had happened, and had gone into hiding.

Waritjanpleng, who was thirty years old and the nephew of Jirawat Sophanworagul, the owner of Choke Charoen fishing pier, had voluntarily turned himself in to the Ranong Provincial Police. Authorities charged him with 'having knowledge of foreigners illegally entering the country, providing them with shelter so they could avoid arrest, and carelessness leading to their deaths'.

Chalhermchai claimed that his uncle, Jirawat, was not involved in the incident, nor was Chalhermchai's wife Panchalee. Police believed Panchalee to be the woman who had counted the Burmese migrants before they entered the truck, and had issued a warrant for her arrest.

Chalhermchai went on to say that he was given 20,000 baht by Supat Phothong to let human traffickers use his uncle's pier. Supat, he continued, was a labor broker who took orders from native Thai's for Burmese workers. Although Chalhermchai denied any other wrongdoing in the case, police did not believe him. They had been told by others in custody that it was Chalhermchai who had not only let the traffickers use the pier, but had also been responsible for loading the migrants into the truck. In addition, he had been the one to open and close the doors on a warehouse, allowing the truck to enter and exit the building.

After learning of what had happened to the migrants in the back of the truck, Chalhermchai claimed that he had fled to Pattani, alone, and hidden there until turning himself in. He insisted that after the news broke he and his wife had gone their separate ways, even though she had no involvement in the smuggling of the workers. Although he would not tell authorities where she was, he promised them that he would have his wife turn herself in the next day.

But instead of waiting, thirty-five year old Panchalee Chusuk contacted authorities that same day and offered to surrender, telling them that she was eager to prove her innocence.

Questioned at the home of Ranong Police Chief Apirak Hongthong, Panchalee denied counting the migrants as they boarded the truck, and only admitted to keeping track of those passing through the warehouse where the truck was parked. She had only done this, she stressed, so she could prepare packets of food for them.

She then insisted that neither her husband, nor his uncle, Jirawat, had any involvement in the crime. She and her husband had fled to Pattani after hearing the news, simply out of fear, and had hidden out at the home of a relative. Authorities did not fail to note that this statement completely contradicted her husbands, who had said that he and his wife had gone their separate ways.

Now, eight days after the discovery of the fifty-four dead migrants, police had all the suspects involved in custody, save one. Only Supat Phothong, the thirty-four year old man believed to be the broker who brought the Burmese migrants to Thailand, had escaped capture. The others were held at the Ranong prison, awaiting trial, and denied bail.

****

The public and the news media were still clamoring for those involved in the 'death truck incident' to be tried on human trafficking charges, but by mid-April, that idea was put to rest once and for all.

On April 21, 2008, Immigration Police Commander Lieutenant General Chatchaw al Suksomjit held a press conference to confirm that there was not enough evidence to charge those involved with human trafficking. Instead, he told the waiting press, the six Thai Nationals would be charged with death by negligence, and could receive a maximum sentence of ten years for each person who had died.

Although disgusted, the public took some consolation in the thought that those responsible might be serving 540 years in prison.

****

At the same time, the survivors of the tragedy were learning the penalty they would have to pay for having been subjected to such a horrific ordeal.

Fourteen were minors, and immediately deported back to Burma without facing charges, and two others were not charged because they were still trying to recover in a Thailand hospital. That left the remaining fifty to face trial and learn their punishment.

All were convicted of illegal entry into the country, and sentenced to ten days in jail. In addition, each was fined 2,000 baht, and deported back to Burma.

But they had gotten off easy. After all, they were facing a two-month prison sentence, but the sympathetic Thailand courts only gave them ten days.

Afterword

The suffocation death of 54 Burmese migrant workers in the back of a sealed container did more to bring attention to the crime of human trafficking, and the plight of its victims, than any other event before or since. Yet human trafficking continues to occur, and it remains a thriving business.

There have been several discrepancies in the story told by both survivors of this tragedy and those who witnessed it. Some say the people were forced to ride in the truck standing up, and that the truck had been stopped on the side of the road for more than an hour, waiting for a military checkpoint to close for the night. Others claimed that the air conditioner did not break down, but that Bunplong shut it off deliberately, while some insist the driver never unlocked the doors before he fled. They claim it was nearby villagers who heard their cries for help and finally freed them.

The entire truth of what actually happened in the 'Ranong Human Trafficking Death Truck' will probably never be known. All one can hope is that those 54 people did not die in vain, and that their death can be a lesson the world will learn from.

Those who had high hopes that the perpetrators of the ordeal might receive as much as 540 years in prison, as authorities had claimed, were sorely disappointed when the trials were complete. Of the seven people suspected to be involved in the 'death truck incident', five were convicted of gross negligence and breaking immigration laws and their sentences ran as follows:

Damrong Phussadee, who owned the truck, received ten years in prison.

Jirawat Sophapanworagul, the owner of the Choke Charoen fishing pier received a sentence of six years.

Chalhermchai Waritjanpleng, who received money for letting the traffickers use his uncle's pier, was sentenced to nine years.

Panchalee Chusuk, Chalhermchai's wife, who counted the migrants as they boarded the truck, originally received a six-year term, but this was subsequently reduced to three years.

Suchon Bunplong, the driver of the truck who disregarded the immigrant's pleas for help, received twelve years, but because he had confessed to trafficking illegal aliens, his sentence too was cut in half and he was ordered to do six years.

It is unknown whether authorities ever picked up Supat Phothong; the alleged broker who procured the 120 Burmese migrants for those Thai's who had ordered them. Although police had issued a warrant for his arrest, as of this date, he apparently has not been tried.

The same goes for Weera Dum Yingyaud, who was arrested, but as of now has not gone to trial. It could not be determined whatever became of him, and it is possible that he was released from custody and the charges against him dropped.

Three of those convicted were immediately released from jail after posting bond of 200,000 to 400,000 baht. They will remain free pending their appeal.

All of the survivors from the back of the seafood truck were repatriated back to Burma, and to the majority of the public, the feeling that they got a raw deal ran high. Even the National Human Rights Commission publicly stated that Thailand had 'treated them shabbily.'

Although what happened to those 120 victims was tragic, they were but a drop in the bucket when you consider the tens of thousands of Burmese migrants who enter Thailand each year. Many of these other migrants die too; the only difference is that their deaths didn't make headlines.

In November of 2007, seven Burmese migrants, along with their Thai taxi driver, were killed when the taxi they were riding in crashed during a high-speed chase to avoid arrest.

In December of that same year, twenty-two more died when the rickety old boat they were being smuggled in capsized, and all were drowned.

Another seven drowned in January while trying to make the crossing into Thailand.

There are many such stories from numerous other illegal immigrants, all of them simply trying to find a better life.

Leaders from all over the world now regularly meet to discuss ways to crack down on human trafficking and prosecute those involved in it. There are conferences held, papers written, seminars attended, and speeches made, yet the answer on how to end this trade is as elusive as ever.

Thailand itself set June 6, 2008 as 'D-Day' for human trafficking, issuing a stricter law on that date to supersede their more lenient one against trafficking. But the crime still exists in the country.

It might be that no matter what governments and law enforcement agencies try to put in place to quell this barbaric crime, it may never be enough. For it is only when all individuals come to realize that every human being has worth, value, and the right to be treated with decency and respect that the human trafficking trade will cease to exist.

Bibliography

www.ide.go.jp/Englis/Publish/Download/DP/pdf/2
57.pdf

myanmarhumantrafficking.gov.mm/content/faqs

www.worldvision.com.au/issues/humantrafficking

www.phuketgazette.net/news/details.asp?fromse
arch=yes&id=6397&search=driver

Phuketwan.com/tourism/horror-of-human-trade-
54-die-in-Phuket-bound-container/

www.thedailybeast.com/newsweek/2008/04/12/l
ured-into-bondage.html

www.phuketgazette.net/archives/articles/2008/article6402.html

teakdoor.com/Thailand-and-asia-news/27304-54-burmese-job-seekers-soffocate-ranonh-2.html

www.foxnews.com/printer_friendly_wires/2008apr16/0,4675,thailandsuffocationdeaths,00.html

whatismatt.com/the-trouble-with-burmese-migrants/

www.alipac.us/f12/thailand-driver-thai-truck-tragedy-surrenders-105877/

www.upi.com/top_news/2008/04/16/surrender-in-deadly-migrant-smuggling/upi-566312083771

www.asiaviews.org/regional-news-a-specials-report/22393-reportalias3568?tmpl=component&print=1&page=

teakdoor.com/593322-postl.html

www.phuketgazette.net/news/savedf.php?ref=20131170538&id=19835

phuketgazette.net/archives/articles/2008/articles6241.html

updates.theworldrace.org/?filename=all-about-thailand

www.humantrafficking.org/countries/thailand

www.mekongmigration.org/mmn/?p=70

www.no-trafficking.org/content/press_rooms_pdf/thai%20fm%20said_mcot_17_08.pdf

www.cesd.soc.cmu.ac.th/2012/en/news.php?cmd=detail&id=2039

usatoday30.usatoday.com/news/world/2008-04-09-2857217462-x.htm

twocircles.net/node/66132

www.ingramcontent.com/pod-product-compliance
Lightning Source LLC
Chambersburg PA
CBHW070550290526
45790CB00002B/629